EPOXY RESIN ART

__ for Beginners __

The Most Amazing Resin Creations with Step-by-Step Instructions and Images to Follow | How to Make Lamps, Tables, Jewelry, Dioramas, and More!

CONTENTS

INTRODUCTION

Have you ever encountered those DIY epoxy resin tutorials and asked yourself, "Can I make that?" Well, why not? Though most people think epoxy art is for professionals only, I believe anyone can pick up the right tools and products and create a masterpiece.

To create epoxy art, you will need a list of good and practical ideas to experiment with. Learning to make new things out of epoxy resin was a self-exploration I started a few years ago. Initially, I worked on simpler things like making a bookmark, a pendant, or a coaster to learn this new skill. Today I enjoy making floral resin lamps, tabletops, trays, and all sorts of possible things you can make using epoxy resin. Every time I complete a project, it pumps me to create more. And if you are an enthusiastic crafter like me, I think you will like playing with the resins.

If you want to learn the art of making epoxy resin products from the fundamental level with simple ideas to work on, this guidebook is the perfect read for you. From getting the right resin to making, preparing, pouring, and setting resin, I have shared all the necessary details a beginner must know before starting. So read on and find out more.

Chapter 1:
What is Epoxy Resin?

Resin art is a creative medium to experiment with, regardless of your experience level. All you need to get started is a few supplies and an awareness of how they will enable you to produce some great masterpieces. Let your creativity run wild and delve deeply into resin art's brand-new, limitless world.

Resin art has, surprisingly, been around for a very long time. As trees produce, amber is nature's resin and fossilizes to form a solid, clear slab.

Decorative jewelry and ornaments made of amber have been used for hundreds of years. Modern resin is produced artificially and utilized for the same purposes.

In the 1930s, epoxy resin was first identified as a product used in arts and crafts. It was patented as a separate product once individuals realized it could be used to preserve stuff or hold things together. The epoxy resin then found its way into the art world, which has been in great use ever since.

When a resin-carrying tree trunk is poked, the liquid inside pops out, which turns into resin, a very viscous substance. When these oils are exposed to air, they oxidize and become resin – a thick, gooey substance. Natural resin has been utilized since ancient Greece, when it was widely used as an early type of chewing gum to keep one's breath fresh. The epoxy resin we now use to make an artwork combines two products: synthetic polymer resin and a hardener. They come separately in a container, and when combined, they go through a chemical reaction that causes the mixture to harden and create a solid product.

The total amount of the prepared epoxy resin you need for a particular project can be calculated by analyzing the dimensions. An online calculator allows you to enter the dimension of the required resin product, and it tells you how much resin is required to get those dimensions. The ratio of resin to hardener in resin art is typically 1:1. Prioritize precisely measuring and carefully combining the ingredients to get a fully cured and long-lasting product.

One of the most intriguing creative mediums to deal with is epoxy resin, which can be used to create 2D and 3D works of art. The epoxy resin adds to or seals your works in acrylic pouring, giving them more depth and vibrancy. Even though there are many incredible techniques to try while experimenting with epoxy resin art, it might be scary at first, especially if you don't know how to work with it. Epoxy resin art techniques aren't as complex as you imagine until you get the hang of them. Understanding the various uses for epoxy resin can enhance your use of it and open new possibilities for improving your finished products.

Chapter 2:
Tools Needed

Before you select a **DIY** project to start working on, make sure to get all the supplies needed for that project. Though every project will call for epoxy resin, you will have to get the one most suitable for the look of your artwork. Besides the resin, you will need several things and tools to complete your project. For those planning to get their hands dirty with the resin artwork, I recommend setting up a proper working station per the safety guidelines I have shared in this chapter and keeping all the following tools and supplies.

Epoxy Resin

Depending on the scale of your project, Epoxy resin products come in a range of quantities from 8 oz to 10 gallons. If you are uncertain about the amount required, you can easily determine how much resin you need and which kit to purchase by calculating the dimensions of the project.

Gloves

Use disposable gloves to protect your hands. Epoxy resin is sticky when liquid; thus, wearing gloves will keep your hands clean and prevent potential skin irritation. When working with resin, ensure you have several pairs of gloves. I prefer nitrile gloves since they are much stronger and hypoallergenic even though they resemble latex gloves. Nitrile gloves are available at online stores, and you may also find a pair in a resin art kit.

Apron or Old Clothes

Wear an apron, a smock, or old clothes while working to prevent resin drips from damaging your clothes. Getting it off can be challenging if any resin drips onto your clothing. To keep the epoxy resin out, it is also recommended to tie your hair or keep it covered if you have long hair.

Plastic Drop Sheet

Use a plastic sheet to shield your work surface and floor from resin spills or drips. Resin drips can be cleaned with paper towels and isopropyl alcohol, or, if allowed to dry, they can be scraped off the next day. A clear, smooth vinyl shower curtain offers a cheap, durable liner that can be used repeatedly to protect the working surface. Kitchen parchment paper is also an excellent option for quick cleaning.

Masking Tape

Suppose you wish to resin the sides of an art piece. You can tape off the bottom with high-quality painter's tape, which will help prevent drips from ruining your artwork at the center. Due to gravity, drips will build up around the bottom as the resin flows down the sides. The tape will catch these drips, and after the resin is dry enough to touch, you can remove the tape and the drips along with it.

Stands

Excess resin can collect on the plastic-lined work surface when plastic stands to support your item. I like to use painter's pyramid supports; you can purchase them separately or as part of your accessory kit. You can get them in the paint area of any hardware store. Large toy construction blocks or plastic shot glasses also work nicely; both can be purchased at a dollar shop.

Level

Use a regular level to make sure your work is horizontal. If your piece is tilted, epoxy will run off the sides at the lowest place, ruining everything.

Plastic Container for Water Bath

If the resin you're working with is cold, a warm water bath will reheat it to room temperature and make it easier to handle. Choose a narrow container with high sides to prevent the bottles from toppling. The capped bottles should be soaked in warm water for 10 to 15 minutes after filling them halfway. You can now measure the resin and hardener and mix them in a container.

Stir Stick

Improperly mixed resin won't cure properly, so be sure to scrape the sides and bottom of the container while you stir. A smooth stick is good for mixing all the resin and hardeners in a container. Unlike spherical items (like spoons), a stir stick with a flat side can scrape the container more effectively. Ice-cream sticks made of wood can also be used, but they must be thrown away after each use.

Mixing Container

Using a cup with clearly visible measurement markings is crucial to saving you from guesstimating while measuring and mixing resin because improperly measured resin and hardener do not cure well. As long as both are precisely measured in the stated amounts, it doesn't matter which part is poured into which part. Whether you measure the resin or the hardener first, they both must be in equal proportion for the resin to cure. You can reuse your mixing cups for each session.

Spreader

Epoxy resin will naturally self-level when you pour it into or onto a surface, but a flat plastic spreader distributes it uniformly over your work. To direct the resin, use a plastic spreader with a flat edge. Spreaders are typically included in epoxy resin art kits, so you won't need to purchase them individually. You can also use a wooden popsicle stick, a toothpick, or an old paintbrush to put Epoxy resin where you want it to go if you simply want to cover a portion of your item. A small spatula or a plastic takeout knife works well to push the resin up to the edge without spilling over. It also works well if you'd like the resin to sit perfectly in a dome on top of your artwork without going over the sides. You can also use a foam brush or gloved hands to apply resin to the sides of your item.

Torch

A flame torch is the finest method for obtaining a flawless, bubble-free finish. Numerous bubbles are produced when the resin is mixed; if not eliminated, these bubbles will stay even after the cure time of your artwork. They cannot be removed by blowing into a straw or pricking with a toothpick. Hairdryers don't work as well since they cannot reach a hot enough temperature to get rid of the bubbles. They also puff air out with pressure, blowing the resin around and adding dust to the artwork. So, a tiny butane torch works well for most of the project. You can also use a hot gun if necessary because alcohol is flammable. For larger objects, a propane torch is the best option! Any hardware store has butane and propane refill for this torch.

Toothpicks

When resining, toothpicks are a must-have. After torching your art piece, hold it to the light at eye level to check for stray bubbles and any hair or dust particles. A toothpick can move tiny amounts of resin or precisely position add-ons like gold flakes or jewels.

Dust Cover

Before beginning to resin, prepare a temporary cover since you never want to leave your newly resined artwork exposed while searching for a cardboard box or plastic tote. Ensure the cover is cleaned to prevent dust from falling into your wet art piece. Plastic totes make a good cover as they are simple to clean. Or you can use a cardboard box, but make sure the flaps are removed. Ensure that the cover is large enough to cover the entire artwork and that none of its internal surfaces touch the wet resin inside.

Alcohol and Paper Towel

For spills and cleanup, paper towels and isopropyl alcohol are used. Wipe the wet resin off the surface with paper towels first, then spritz your tools with alcohol to eliminate any leftover residue. Once there is no residue, wipe dry with additional paper towels. When all resin residue has been removed from your instruments, wash them in hot, soapy water and let them dry completely before using them again.

Hand Cleaner

If you get Epoxy resin on your skin, wash it off immediately to avoid potential skin irritation. You can also clean sticky hands with an exfoliating hand cleaner; in this case, the hardware store's exfoliating hand cleanser is excellent. You can alternatively dry rub your hands to remove the resin using a few poppyseeds, salt, and liquid soap. After that, give your hands a good rinse with water.

Silicone Molds

Silicone molds are ideal for small resin art projects since they are flexible and easy to remove from the resin surface, unlike rigid plastic molds that could rip or distort the set resin. You can use them repeatedly because they return to their original shape. Molds come in almost every size and shape, and you can buy any depending upon the requirement of your project. You may add inclusions like beer caps, shells, colorful stones, gems, crystals, and much more to silicone molds. They are easy to wash and clean for reuse.

Colorants

When colored, epoxy resin has a lovely appearance; for optimal effects, always use a colorant made especially for resin, such as Resin Tint liquid colorant. Once the resin and the hardener are well mixed together in a container, add the colorant.

Plastic Cups

Plastic cups are great for mixing resin with different colors simultaneously. You can use popsicle sticks and clear plastic drinking glasses to do this. The resin needed for your project should be combined in one large batch. Depending on how much resin you need for each color, portion it into separate cups. For each hue, use a different cup. Drop the tint into the resin and thoroughly blend it until the resin has a single, unified color. You can always add additional color if you start with less than you think you need. Pulling a small amount of tinted resin up the side of the plastic cup will allow you to gauge the color's depth; if more tint is required, add it now. Just remember, the resin should be divided into separate plastic cups, one for each hue.

Wood Panels and Metal Trays

Epoxy resin is heavy; thus, wood panels are a perfect choice when dealing with resin. Strong substrates hold the weight of resin the best. When pouring colored resin for flow art or ocean art, cradled wood panels are an excellent choice since they have a lip to hold the resin. Metal serving dishes are also excellent for this use.

Heat Gun and Hair Dryer

Use a hair dryer for flow art and a heat gun for silicone molds; while we almost always advise using a flame torch, there are three exceptions. When using alcohol ink, be aware that alcohol is flammable, and using a flame torch could result in a fire. In most cases, the alcohol in ink will dissolve many resin bubbles, but a heat gun is suggested if you require more assistance. It is a useful substitute for a flame torch, especially when dealing with silicone molds, because a flame's intensity risks destroying the mold's surface. To make cells and lacing for flow art or ocean art, use a low setting on a hair dryer or heat gun to gently press the layers of colored resin together. And to quickly remove any bubbles from the surface, use a flame torch to complete the process.

Inclusions

To add shine and texture, you can add crystals, gold leaf, decorative stones, charms, glitter, and other decorative items to your work. "Inclusions" is a fancy word for all the adorable little decorations you can add to your resin artwork. You can suspend gold leaf flakes, add crushed glass or crystals in the resin, add glitter for brightness and depth, or make coasters out of dried flowers, shells, or bottle caps. There are a gazillion things at the craft store that you can add to your resin artwork. Always ensure your inclusions are completely dried; we recommend testing beforehand to ensure you get the desired outcome.

Sandpaper

Sandpaper is used to rub the surface of the cured resin and give it a fine finish. It is also great for scrapping unwanted dust or hair stuck on the surface of the resin artwork. You can use a piece of coarse sandpaper (such as 80 grit), a sanding block, or an electric sander over the entire surface. Pay special attention to sanding out the things you want to remove. It will appear to be a mess, but don't worry. It will look as good as new once you remove all of the sanding dust and apply a coat of resin polish over the surface.

Chapter 3:
How to Choose the Right Resin

There are just so many resins that, for a newbie, it is almost impossible to decide which resin to get and which one is best for a particular project. Let me tell you one thing here; there is no one-size-fits-all formula for picking a resin. The different varieties of resin are used differently and serve other purposes. So, before you hit the stores and walk from aisle to aisle to find that perfect resin product, here is a list of factors you should look at and learn about.

Type of Artwork

Do you want to pour the resin into a mold, in between surfaces, or to fill something, or do you want a resin to cover the tabletops, wall clock base, serving trays, or other flat surfaces? The answer to this question is the factor that helps you pick the right resin. For filling and casting projects, thin resins are the best, whereas the thicker resin varieties are more suitable for doming or covering the surface.

Viscosities

There are degrees of viscosity that you need to know about. The degree of flow resistance in a liquid is described by its viscosity. The viscosity in the context of epoxy resin formulae dictates whether the substance will drip or spread uniformly and whether it should be poured, dipped, or painted on the substance. The physical qualities created and how much epoxy perforates the substrate are both influenced by viscosity. There are two main types of viscosities when it comes to epoxy resin. The viscosity level determines the projects you can use epoxy for.

<u>Low Viscosity</u>

Resin with low viscosity takes a very long duration to cure. While using a low viscosity resin, you can manage longer gaps between the processing steps. So they are perfect for beginners because they give you more time to learn and experiment. The low-viscosity epoxy resin typically takes 12 to 24 hours to set. Relatively little heat is released from the slow exothermic chemical transformation process. Therefore, unlike high- or medium-viscosity epoxy resins, thicker layers and larger amounts of the material can be treated without any issues in a single session.

High Viscosity

Due to their stiff consistency, the high viscosity of epoxy resins is similar to honey. The products in this category are exceptionally well suited for covering surfaces and are frequently used for laminating purposes. They can also be used for projects like making resin geodes and art. Take the manufacturer's recommendations for mixing the two parts of this resin, and remember that they have a shorter cure time, so you would have to work quickly to handle these resins.

Pot Time

When working with epoxy resins, the so-called processing time is a crucial consideration. Some people refer to it as pot time. These words indicate the time window between mixing the two components and processing the resin (resin and hardener). Eventually, a phase sets in during which the resin thickens and becomes more viscous. It shouldn't be processed any further at this point because it won't level out to a flat surface on its own and can't be colored evenly. Beginners are advised to consider low-viscosity resins, which have a longer pot time, so they can mix them easily without any worries.

Demold Time

The demold time is the duration in which the resin that is poured into a mold partially hardens, just enough to be taken out of the mold. Once demolded, the art piece is left to cure more according to the stated time on the product label. The resin with a short demold time helps you use one mold repeatedly.

Cure Time

It is the time duration that a well-mixed resin takes after mixing to harden completely. The cure time is different for each product, and if you are a beginner, you should look for a resin with a longer curing time so that you can easily mix and pour the resin into the desired mold without the fear of it hardening quickly. The cure time is mentioned on the resin bottle, and you can pick and choose after reading into it. Most epoxy resins we use for artwork have a curing time of 24 hours. So once poured, such resins much be checked the next day for the results. The curing time of a resin depends on the thickness of the resin layer; you may want to leave the resin to cure for 6-7 days if it is a resin table or a similar product that you are making.

FDA Compliance

If you want to make resin products that will be used to serve or keep food (like resin bowls, serving trays, or plates), then always choose the resin that meets the FDA compliance standards. Such types of resin come with a label stating that the product (when fully cured) does not contaminate the food it touches.

UV Protection

Resins with UV protection tend to stay good as new for a longer duration, and they don't get yellow too soon. That is why I recommend buying the ones with UV protection labels.

ASDM Certification Safety Standards

If you live in the United States, you should look for the "ASDM" certification label on the resin product you buy. This label indicates that your product meets the government safety standards and is safe to use according to the given instructions on the label. The government safety regulations are named differently in other countries, and you should look for the respective safety certification of your country if you are living out of the States.

Chapter 4:
Safety Precautions

Compared to working with ordinary paint and sealer, working with epoxy resin art techniques is more difficult and poses unique challenges. It is an exothermic chemical reaction that you initiate every time you mix a resin with a hardener. So dealing with these chemicals is not safe unless you take the necessary precautions. The fumes are released, and when continuously inhaled, they may affect your breathing or cause an allergic reaction in some people. That is why it is recommended to follow the safety precautions below.

Use Protective Gear

Wearing protective clothing whenever working with resin is the first thing to remember. I cannot stress this enough. When working with resin, safety equipment is crucial. Avoid working with resin if you don't have the necessary safety equipment until you do. While some resin products are advertised as non-toxic, most hardeners still contain chemical elements that might irritate the throat if inhaled. The resin sticks to porous surfaces like skin and hair like super glue and can occasionally call for a trip to the hospital to be removed. Resin fumes and particles from sanding resin might cause lung problems. Everyone's respiratory systems are different; even if your best friend, the artist, has worked with resin without protection his entire life with no problems, you still need to proceed with caution.

You will also need safety goggles because the resin can irritate your eyes. How might I get resin in my eye, you might be wondering. Artists work the resin with a straw in various pouring techniques to create multiple designs. Sometimes, the splattering from these straws results in resin getting into your eye, acting as a superglue. If your eyes are not protected, resin particles from sanding might severely irritate them. While working with resin, you'll be safe using a respirator, safety goggles, and disposable non-porous gloves.

Use a Respirator

You may have heard that using epoxy resin requires a respirator. This is accurate for many resin brands available today. Keeping a respirator in your workstation is overall good for your health. You can use it not only for resin projects but also for other projects which need to release dust and toxins into the environment. There is no harm in inhaling pure air while working; caution is always better. So, make sure to get a respirator for yourself.

Work in a Place with Good Ventilation

Even if you have access to a ventilator, your workspace or studio should have windows that are simple to open so that hazardous gases can escape. I do not advise working with resin if you do not have access to a room with windows or a suitable ventilation system. Fumes from the resin will continue accumulating in your workspace as it cures, and you will continue to breathe them in when returning to check on the artwork. A fan is helpful but does not constitute adequate ventilation without sucking air from your workstation outdoors. Adding an oscillating fan won't do much other than disseminate the odors around your house. Your workplace needs to be well ventilated to protect you and your family.

Keep Pets and Kids Away

Resin particles can easily contaminate food and beverages, which can cause poisoning or other gastrointestinal problems. Avoid working at a place where there is a pet nearby. The fumes from curing resin are as harmful to the animal's lungs as it is to humans. Animals are susceptible to the same risks you do while working with unprotected resin. Besides pets, keep little children away from your studio.

Cleaning Tips

If you accidentally get resin on your skin, I developed a way to remove it from your hands without using harmful chemicals. When working with epoxy resin, I always advise wearing the appropriate PPE. Still, if you've ever accidentally gotten some on your skin, you know how sticky and virtually hard it is to get off!

Here's how to remove resin from your hands successfully with natural ingredients:

- Immediately dispense one tablespoon of baking soda into your hand. There is no need to wet your hands with water.
- Add dishwashing soap to the baking soda.
- Over a sink, scrub your hands well.
- After scrubbing for 1-2 minutes, rinse off this mixture with water.
- Repeat the same cleaning steps if necessary.

Chapter 5:
Processing of Epoxy Resin

There is a complete science behind the working of the epoxy resin. Mixing a resin with its hardener gives us a solidified product; sure, we all know this! But resin art is all about how we process resin before it solidifies.

There are many types of resin art, but before we get into that, let's explain the whole process first.

Resin Casting

Casting is pouring a liquid substance into a mold so it can harden over time. You can use silicone molds of almost any size or type with resin casting; even candy silicone molds are useful in this regard. Resin casts get firm enough to remove from the mold within 12 to 24 hours, depending on the size of your project, and after demolding, they should be cured within a few days. Silicone molds in different shapes and sizes are widely available online and offline. You can also buy kits or create your mold depending on the requirement of a particular project.

Pouring Resin

This method involves pouring nicely combined resin and hardener onto a flat or three-dimensional surface. The goal is to cover an existing surface and cast to create a new surface. Almost any surface that is compatible with resin can be used to produce resin pour artwork, including a blank canvas, an old table, a laminated photo that you wish to use as a keychain, or even ornamental tiles.

Polyethylene plastic, silicone, waxy surfaces, painter's tape, or materials like wax or freezer paper are common surfaces to which resin won't adhere, so you can use those surfaces to set the resin into a particular shape and then remove them once it solidifies.

Within 24 hours, your resin piece hardens enough to move, then is fully cured in a few days. Always follow the manufacturer's instructions to avoid a sticky, uncured mess. Though every resin project is different in the way it is created, and a unique combination of supplies is used for each, there are a few simple guidelines that can be applied to any resin artwork that'll result in a masterpiece.

Mixing and Preparing the Resin

Prepare your work area first, then assemble all your equipment and cover the table you'll be using with freezer paper. If you need to move your resin to cure for 24 hours, I recommend covering a baking pan with freezer paper so you can easily move your molds. You need to work in a well-ventilated location. When it comes to drying time, resin doesn't give you a lot of leeways, so once you get going, you won't want to dash off to get some glitter. Grab everything you'll need right away. Then put your respirator on so you can start working.

First, prepare the mold or surfaces you need for a project. When everything is ready, start mixing the hardener with the resin. Mostly they are combined in 1:1 proportion, but you must follow the mixing instructions given on the resin bottle you are using. Mix the two in a plastic container and mix with a popsicle stick. It's crucial to make sure that your resin is correctly blended. For beginners, I advise attaching a mixer to a drill so you can mix quickly. Use a brand-new mixer if you're using clear resin to prevent color contamination. Usually, your mixer can be used again after adding color to resin. Make sure you have nitrile gloves on before you begin the mixing.

Once thoroughly mixed, the mixture heats a little because of the chemical reaction, which is entirely normal. Once mixed, you can use the transparent resin liquid or add colors to it if needed.

How to Color the Resin

Colors are added to the transparent resin to give it the desired look. For instance, shades of blue pigments are added while making an underwater diorama to give a watery look. Similarly, pigments are added to resin tables or lamps.

Here is what you need to do to make your resin look colored.

Avoid Oil and Water-Based Paints

Using leftover water or oil colors to color the epoxy could be tempting if you already have any on hand. Avoid doing this because paints that are water- or oil-based interfere with the curing process of the resin, and they may ruin the whole reaction. Remember that adding anything could make resin stop reacting as the chemical reaction that produces it requires a precise chemical formula.

Epoxy Liquid Paints

You can add liquid paints to the epoxy resin kit or buy them separately. With these, you may achieve excellent results and lovely, even coloring. Basically, your epoxy will get one uniform, single flat hue throughout. This is ideal if that is the aesthetic you are going for.

Powdered Colors

Rich, deep colors are produced using pigment powders. They won't blend in as smoothly or uniformly as liquid pigments, which can sound terrible but is a good thing as that adds a certain effect to the resin. It produces subtle color variations that enhance the product's visual appeal. You will obtain a hue that varies in intensity from one point to another, fading from bright to dark, royal to light, and more, instead of one shade of color. Mica powder is typically the most effective product used to color epoxy. It is a naturally occurring mineral with a metallic sheen. These powders are created by pulverizing mica and adding color to it.

If the color you just poured isn't giving your item the effect you were hoping for, then don't be disheartened. Remember that each piece of resin art is unique, and you never know what creation can emerge from what you pour, whether you are creating it to sell or give away. Just go with the flow and let your artwork take on a life of its own! Art is for peace of mind, so instead of obsessing over getting the right product, just enjoy the process of making it. Trust me, that helps make wonderful masterpieces.

How Much Pigment to Use

Keep in mind that the chemical reaction required to create epoxy can be disrupted by adding too much of any ingredient, which will prevent the epoxy from properly curing. Because they are highly concentrated and require a very small amount to achieve the desired color, powder pigments are superior to paints and dyes in many ways. According to standard guidelines, the pigment should comprise 2-6% of the mixture's total weight. A digital scale is the most accurate tool for measuring this. If the percentage is less than 2%, the epoxy may not be sufficiently colored. And if it is higher than 6%, then you risk preventing the epoxy's curing reaction. If you want more color, start from 2%, then gradually add more if required. I usually add drops of pigments while pouring the resin into layers; it helps me get the desired result. Just squeeze Alcohol Ink drops into mixed Epoxy resin in a silicone mold to create tendrils, squiggles, and other fascinating effects. Then, with a white Ink Sinker, press the colors down through the resin.

Pouring, Molding, and Casting

An epoxy pour may be used for many applications, including revamping a serving dish and covering an existing painting. Pour gradually, then add heat to remove the bubbles. To diffuse any bubbles that may have formed, it also helps to combine the resin and hardener in one cup before slowly pouring the mixture into a different, clean cup.

Pour your resin slowly when you're ready to do so. Bubbles will develop if the resin is poured too quickly. Pour the resin directly into the mold after you've thoroughly mixed it. Make sure the resin fills the mold's corners by spreading out. You can use your popsicle stick to push the resin against the mold's edges if necessary. Once you have filled the mold with resin, gently tap it a few times to help any air bubbles rise to the top. When pouring resin into a thick project, stop every few seconds and tap the mold.

Put your safety gear on before you start working, then shield your workspace with plastic, a silicone mat, or another impenetrable layer of protection. Avoid using paper or cardboard as a lot of resin may seep through and fuse the materials to the surface underneath the piece.

There is a wide selection of silicone molds available in the stores. Try to buy silicone kits that can be used for resin artwork, soap making, or other crafts you like. This saves your money and gives you various options to work with. Two finishes of silicone are typically available in the market, and those are matte and glossy. Both are compatible with resin, but It's crucial to remember that a rigid mold, like an ice cube tray, won't give you good results while dealing with resin. When removing the set and cured resin from the mold, you need to exert a lot of force to damage any part of the resin, which is impossible if the mold has rigid sides.

Removing Bubbles

Mixing the resin with its hardener tends to trap the surface air particles, creating tiny bubbles in the mixture. Then when you pour this mixture into a mold or onto a surface, more air traps to make more bubbles. These bubbles do not give a fine look to a cured resin piece unless you make a fishbowl necklace, so you must remove the bubbles from the resin before it's too late.

Here are some time-tested bubble-removing techniques that you can use:

Warm Your Resin

Even if it may not be the quickest, it is the safest method for removing bubbles from resin without harming your workpiece. Direct heat through an open flame can damage the resin surface. In contrast, ambient heat manipulates resin's chemical makeup-less dramatically and makes it much easier to maintain its shape. You can keep the mold with the resin in a warmer place and let the bubble escape slowly on its own with time.

Using a Torch

The best way to eliminate bubbles from dry epoxy is with a torch. Keep the torch at a distance from the resin and just pass it over to lightly heat the bubbles. They will escape from the resin upon receiving the heat.

Mix Your Resin and Hardener Well

If you've ever prepared scrambled eggs, you would know that if you use a fork or a whisk, bubbles will form on the surface of the egg mixture. The same thing occurs when resin and hardener are combined too quickly. So make sure to mix them slowly and pour slowly to avoid air bubbles getting into the mixture.

Use a Heat Gun

The best method for removing resin bubbles is to use a heat gun. If you want a cheap yet effective solution to this problem, a heat gun costs about $10 at most craft stores or online shops that you can use. Use this tool after mixing your resin and hardener. Just turn on the heat gun and pass it over the resin reasonably to see all those pesky air bubbles vanish. Heat makes the little bubbles in the resin expand and pop, leaving it nice and clear to pour into your mold.

Add Inclusions!

After pouring the resin, it's time to add inclusions if needed. Inclusions include anything other than resin added to the liquid to give a certain outlook. For instance, adding a miniature fish, glitter, confetti, miniature plants, etc., are different ways to add inclusions. Once your resin is in the mold, all of these things can be placed into it. Using a toothpick or pointed chopstick, you can easily place and adjust the inclusions in their desired position; before adding silicone or plastic-made inclusions like miniature things, clean and dry them properly. You can either add the inclusion to the resin liquid or place the inclusion in the mold and then pour the resin into it. After adding any inclusion, make sure to tap the mold gently.

Let It Cure

When everything is set inside a mold, on a surface, or in a casting, your work will be done, and you will have to leave the resin to harden on its own. Don't try to rush when curing your product as it will affect its structure. You can use natural means to support the curing process.

The epoxy hardening process depends on a correct ratio of 1:1 hardener to resin mixture. The same is true if you add other ingredients to the mixture to speed up the process. When it comes to curing time, most epoxies are primarily influenced by temperature and sunlight. The curing time lowers with the increased temperature of the epoxy resin mixture. I generally advise sticking to the curing time recommended on the resin packaging. It is better to let nature do its job and wait for lasting results.

Demolding, Sanding, and Polishing

When working on a casting resin project, you must remove the set resin from the mold after 24 hours. At this point, it has to be just hard enough to move. After this point, the product is left for curing for days. If the project didn't involve molding, then no demolding is required. Just let the artwork cure as per the given instructions on the resin bottle.

Once completely cured, the resin product has to be scrubbed with sandpaper for a proper finish, and then it is polished for a shinier look. Before you use sandpaper to smooth off your resin piece, spray it with water or submerge it in water to make it moist. Sand the resin's entire surface two or three times. You may achieve a considerably smoother finish on your resin by wet sanding rather than dry sanding. You can also reduce the quantity of dust produced during the sanding process. To prevent inhaling airborne particles as you sand, put on a mask or a respirator.

After finishing the product, you must apply polish over the surface. There are plenty of resin polishes available in the market; invest in the one with the best reviews. Apply the substance freely to cover the resin's entire surface evenly. Use a polishing product that prevents fine scratches for the best results. For instance, products like Turtle Wax Polishing Compound are advertised as having the ability to prevent scratches effectively.

Chapter 6:
Resin Art DIY Projects

1. Resin Letter Keychains

Here is something simple to work on your resin art skills. These keychains are perfect for adding to your keys or gifts to someone special. You can customize the keychains in any possible way by adding the inclusions of your preference.

Materials Required:

- Clear casting epoxy
- Blending ware
- Gloves
- Mixing sticks
- Blue cast-on craft transparent dyes
- Alphabet silicone mold
- Polycolor resin powder
- Resin glitter

How to Make It:

Follow the instructions on the clear casting epoxy packaging to prepare it. Wear disposable gloves and make sure you are working in a well-ventilated location. Mix the resin and hardener in a mixing cup in equal amounts. Pour the resin into a fresh mixing cup after stirring the resin mixture with a stirrer for two minutes. Using a clean stick, stir the resin once more for one or two more minutes. Add a couple of drops of resin color and a good amount of glitter.

Slowly pour the resin into the letter mold. Use a lighter or straw to burst any bubbles that rise to the surface. Give the resin 24 hours to cure. When the resin is tacky enough, you will know it is time to remove it from the mold.

To create a key chain with two different shades of colors, divide the combined resin into two cups, then add two varieties of colors and glitters to the two cups. Alternately pour a small amount of each resin hue into the mold until it is filled. Let the resin cure for 24 hours or more.

Drill a small hole at the top of the letters using a small drill bit. Attach a keychain by threading a big jump ring through the letters' hole. The **DIY** resin letter keychains can now be attached to anything you like.

2. Seashore Resin Jewelry

This seashore jewelry project is a refreshing piece of art you can create for yourself or the people you love. Here I am sharing the idea of making a pendant, but you can incorporate the same idea into making other pieces of jewelry, like a resin ring or earrings.

Materials Required:

- Watercolor paper

- Watercolor paint and paintbrush

- Oval and round jewelry bezels

- Ultra-seal or a water-based sealer

- Small metal sea creatures charms

- White decorative sand

- Jewelry epoxy resin

- Measuring cups, stir sticks, gloves

How to Make It:

On watercolor paper, use a pencil to trace your bezel. Create the appearance of a seashore by using various blue and brown tones. Dry the area. The watercolor painting has to be cut out to fit inside the bezels. You can also print the seashore background painting on paper and cut it out to fit the bezels.

Using water-based glue, stick the cutout into the bezel. Apply the glue to the painting's surface as well. While the glue is still wet, scatter some sand on the coast portion of the image. Place a metal charm along the shoreline using lots of glue. Let this glued bezel dry overnight. To ensure the bezel is level for pouring, place it on an even surface. In a small mixing cup, combine an equal mixture of resin and hardener to get a total volume of 1 oz. Pour mixture into a second little mixing cup after 2 minutes of mixing. For one more minute, stir it well. Slowly pour the resin into the bezel. Although you want a little dome to form on the pendant's surface, take care not to overfill the bezel.

Allow the resin to sit for around 15 minutes, and then use a tiny cooking torch to blow off any surface bubbles. Use a toothpick to remove any larger bubbles, especially those near the metal charm. Give the resin 24 hours to cure undercover. Your bezel is ready to wear.

3. Resin Bookmarks

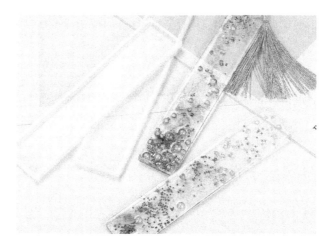

You can make pretty colorful bookmarks using some resin from your craft corner. There are plenty of different ways to style those bookmarks; here, I am using simplest of the method to help you learn the art of making resin bookmarks. There are rectangular silicone molds in the stores that are designed specially to create a bookmark, so you can choose the mold of any desired size to make these.

Materials Required:

- Clear casting epoxy
- Rectangle molds silicone bookmark mold
- Mold release and conditioner
- Glitter
- Metallic/foil confetti
- Mixing cups
- Stir sticks

How to Make It:

Start by combining the resin and hardener in an equal amount. Pour the contents of the first cup into the second and stir for an additional minute with a new stir stick after stirring for two minutes. Add some glitter after mixing it well.

Make sure the mixture is not too thick when you pour it into the molds and fill them up approximately ¼ of the way. After that, you can add more inclusions like metallic confetti, etc. Let them cure for 24 hours, then remove the bookmark from the mold. Drill a little hole at the top of the resin bookmark and attach a tassel of a suitable color. If you buy a mold with space for the hole, you won't have to drill the hole on the bookmark. Your very own bookmark is ready for use.

4. Resin Wood Coasters

Wooden coasters can be coated and covered with a thick layer of transparent or colored resin to give them a 3D look or a colorful effect. Here is a simple method to make wood resin coasters at home.

Materials Required:

- Pour-on epoxy
- Walnut hollow basswood coasters
- Opaque pigments, transparent dyes, and glitter
- Mixing cups and stir sticks
- Gloves, eye protection, surface protection
- Wood coaster supplies

How to Make It:

Add equal parts of the hardener and resin to create 4-6 ounces of resin. Combine 3 ounces of resin and 3 ounces of hardener to make 6 ounces. Read the product's directions for better mixing. Mix the two parts for two minutes to ensure that all the ingredients are blended well, then pour into a new cup. Remix the resin and hardener for a minute or two.

Divide the epoxy into six smaller cups for dying after mixing it per the package's directions. Add a drop of the selected color into each cup of resin. You can also add multiple colors to the epoxy to create a series of colorful resin coasters

Avoid adding too much pigment as this could impact how your resin cures. Add some inclusion into your resin-like pearl color mixed with the blue glitter if you want. To fully incorporate the pigment, stir it with the resin well. Then, pour each resin color over the wood coasters to cover them. I used old plastic cups I wouldn't mind throwing away to lift the wood coasters off the work area. Your coasters' edges will drip with the colors blending. Add more until all of your available colors have been used. To create the marbling effect, pick up each coaster and gently move it back and forth. This will encourage the colors to run together and merge. Drag a stir stick through the colors from one side to the other to make them blend more seamlessly.

To get rid of bubbles that appear on the surface, use a small kitchen torch or a lighter, or simply blow on them with your warm breath. Remove any drips that have developed on the bottom side of the coasters with a stir stick after around 20 minutes. Remove drips and let the resin cure. Before using, give the coasters at least 24 hours to cure.

The finished marbled coasters have such an exquisite look! Because some dyes are more translucent than others, you can still see the wood grains behind some of the marbling and give the coasters the effect of a three-dimensional object. You just cannot achieve the same lovely, marbled appearance with paint. There is no need to seal the high gloss finish, which is lovely. Make some coasters this way, then use the same design to make serving trays, wooden spoon handles, or cutting boards.

5. Resin Confetti Tray

If you want to adorn your coffee table with a colorful tray at the center, here is an amazing and simple idea. For this project, you can take any old wooden tray in your kitchen cabinet and revamp its look using the following supplies.

Materials Required:

- Transparent resin
- Colorful cardstock
- An 8x18 inches Wooden tray
- Mixing cups
- Stir sticks
- Scissors or paper slicer

How to Make It:

Create confetti by cutting colorful paper into tiny bits. Although scissors work just as well, a paper slicer makes this work much easier. After that, add the confetti to your tray. Make sure it is densely piled and covers the bottom evenly. Get ready to pour on the high gloss finish. Do not begin mixing until you are prepared to complete all the steps at once. Mix the resin with its hardener in a mixing cup and stir for 3 minutes.

When the resin is prepared, pour it straight into the tray and completely cover the confetti. Make sure all the paper is wholly coated and add more resin if necessary to get the desired thickness. Use a stirrer to evenly spread the confetti and remove the bubble, if any. Your tray is prepared once the resin is given enough time to cure, which is 2-3 days. You can use the same method to make different other varieties of trays. For example, instead of confetti, you can add glitters, beads, miniature alphabets, etc.

6. Resin Frame with Legos

You can make this amazing colorful frame using some old Legos and the following resin art technique. This frame is a great decoration piece for a kid's room; you can place it on the study table or hang it on the wall.

Materials Required:

- Transparent resin
- Old Wooden frame
- Legos
- Folk-art paint, wicker white
- Respirator
- Gloves
- Cups
- Craft sticks for stirring
- Torch
- 1 ½." painter's tape
- Sandpaper
- Paintbrushes

How to Make It:

Paint your frame with wicker white and let it dry. For mixing, adhere to the directions on the resin container. You should combine 4 oz. of resin.

Starting with measuring out equal portions of resin and hardener, mix mod podge resin (measure by volume, not weight). Each part should be measured in its cup. Pour both parts into a mixing cup after measuring equal amounts of each. Stir the two components together slowly for three minutes. There will be murky swirls when you begin to stir.

To thoroughly combine the two components, scrape the sides and bottom of the mixing cup as you are mixing. Mix the ingredients until the mixture is clear and the foggy swirls have disappeared. Please note that mixing the quantity required for one job at a time is advisable. By applying a small amount of resin on the underside of each Lego and securing it to the frame, attach the Legos. Give it 20 minutes to set. Because you have roughly 30 minutes to work, leave the remaining resin in the cup.

Painter's tape can be used to create a wall around the frame toward the end of the 20 minutes. To prevent glue leaks, press it as hard and closely as you can around the frame. Pour resin over the frame in a thin layer. If any bubbles form, you can remove them using the torch. Give the resin 24 hours to harden, then take the tape off. To round the edges, you can use sandpaper. Make sure to get rid of any dust! To stop the glue from dripping onto the back, tape the frame's back.

Following the directions, combine the remaining resin (or about 4 oz). Once more, cover the entire frame with resin and let it overflow from the edges to cover the sides. Then, allow it to sit for a while before taking the tape off the frame's back. Let the resin fully harden overnight.

7. Blue Glitter Resin Coasters

These blue glitter resin coasters are my personal favorite. I have used the same idea to make several different colored glittered coaster sets for my friends. It doesn't have to be blue; you can choose any color of your liking. Besides glitter, you can golden flakes or dried flowers to the resin to create a different look.

Materials Required:

- 2 oz. clear epoxy resin/ per mold
- Silicone coaster molds
- Cups for pouring and mixing
- Craft sticks or other stir sticks
- Drop cloth
- Clear bumper feet
- Glitter
- Tools

- Gloves

- Respirator

- Timer

- Butane torch

How to Make It:

Mix 2 ounces of resin product in a 1:1 ratio of resin and hardener to make one coaster. While blending for three minutes, scrape the cup's bottom and sides. Divide equally among the three cups. Add a pinch of one type of blue glitter to one cup, another type of blue glitter to another, and yet another type of blue glitter to the third cup. Stir slowly in each cup until the epoxy resin and glitter are thoroughly mixed.

Only a small amount of each color should be poured into the coaster mold at a time. Pour each mixture carefully in a swirling manner. With a stick, gently swirl the colors together after layering them. For two minutes, let it stand. Using a butane torch, carefully remove any bubbles. Repeat after another five minutes. Remove the coaster from the mold once it has dried for 24 hours. Then remove the coasters from their molds and use them whenever needed.

8. Colorful Cupcake Stand

If you don't like your cupcake stand to be plain and white, then don't worry; this colorful stand-top idea is perfect for you. With some well-prepared transparent resin and a handful of sprinkles, you can give your cupcake stand a new look. For a floral look, you can replace sprinkles with some dried flowers. Since flowers are more delicate, make sure to handle them with care.

Materials Required:

- Cake stands with a raised edge
- Super clear resin
- Colorful sprinkles
- Gloves
- Mixing cups
- Stir sticks
- Packing tape

How to Make It:

Prepare roughly 3 ounces of the resin by mixing the resin and hardener per the suggested proportions given on the packaging. Add the colorful sprinkle right into the mixture. The sprinkles should be evenly placed throughout the resin cup. To DIY, make sure your cupcake stand is on a flat surface and that you don't have to move it for roughly 24 hours during the whole curing time. After that, cover your stand with epoxy resin up to the lip of the cake stand. If the stand lacks a lip, pour until it almost reaches the edge. You can see spots with no sprinkles or where the sprinkles are piled on top of one another.

Spread the sprinkles with a stick to ensure that they are uniformly distributed and not piled on top of one another. Check the stand from several perspectives to ensure the sprinkles are flat. Remove any extra resin that reaches the edge or escapes from the lipped surface by wiping it away. Before your resin begins to cure, blow out any bubbles. Give the entire stand at least 24 hours to cure.

As the resin cures, cover the stand with a box to keep dust and other particles out of the resin. You will have a cured stand after 24 hours, but the sprinkles won't be all coated. Make a small wall using paper tape around the edges of the stand to add a second layer of resin to submerge the sprinkle completely. Combine and apply a second resin layer. Create yet another batch of 3 ounces of crystal-clear resin.

Pour until the product overflows the edges of the surface. Make sure all visible surfaces are covered with resin. Before it begins to cure, remove any bubbles. Give the clear epoxy around 45 minutes to cure. Remove the tape from the edge to clean up any resin on other parts of your homemade cupcake stand. Now let it cure for 24 hours. Keep in mind to cover again to avoid contamination. Once the stand has fully cured, you can place cupcakes on the top and serve.

9. DVD Mosaic Resin Tray

It's time to put some DVDs to good use. You can now cut them into pieces to create a lovely mosaic art in a serving tray. This technique can also create mosaic art on a tabletop or a Charcuterie board.

Materials Required:

- 8 by 18 inches wooden tray
- 9-10 old DVDs
- Clear Epoxy resin
- Resin Hot glue/gun
- Scissors

How to Make It:

Start using some sturdy scissors or clippers to cut your DVDs in half. DVDs have two layers, with a metallic foil sandwiched in between. You can gently separate them with your fingertips. After that, cut the halves into tiny pieces. Do not touch the bright metallic surface to avoid leaving fingerprints. Then, use hot glue to attach each piece to the tray's bottom. To fill the space in between the pieces, cut smaller pieces of DVDs accordingly.

For an 18 by 8" tray, you can use 9 DVDs. Try to keep an even spacing around all the tiny "tiles." Use 8 ounces of the prepared resin for this project. Take the time to read and follow the instructions on the bottles properly. Mix the hardener and the resin in a 1:1 ratio. Blend the two parts in one cup for two minutes, then transfer with a different stirring stick into another cup and blend for an additional minute.

After setting the DVD pieces in the tray, pour the resin into the tray and move it gently so that the resin fills the bottom and corners of the tray. If there are any bubbles, remove them by using a heat gun on low heat. Cover it with a cardboard box to stop dust from sticking to the resin's surface. Afterward, wait for 24 hours for the resin to cure. Your mosaic tray is ready to use!

10. Fishbowl Necklace

These fishbowl necklaces are the cutest little things you can create using transparent resin. You will need mini bowl necklaces with a cork and chain on top aside from resin and miniature goldfish.

Materials Required:

- Clear casting epoxy
- Mixing cups
- Measuring cups
- Stir sticks
- Protective gloves
- Mini globe containers with corks
- Eye hooks
- Miniature goldfish
- Necklace chain

How to Make It:

Measure and combine your two parts of epoxy resin first. Wearing safety gloves and carefully following the in-box directions are recommended. Fill half of the mini globe containers with epoxy. When the resin starts to harden, add your fish to the center and arrange it with a stick. This fish might hit the bottom of the mold if you add it too soon. To arrange everything, use needle-nose pliers or a long needle.

Once everything is properly set up, ensure your jars are upright. When the resin has dried, measure more of the resin, mix, and pour again into the molds to fill them. Let the resin cure for 24 hours. After that, screw the eye hooks into the top of the corks. Attach the corks to the bottles' tops to complete your fishbowl necklace and insert a necklace chain. You don't have to leave or remove the bubbles from the resin for this project as it perfectly gives a look of water in a fishbowl!

11. Glittery dominoes

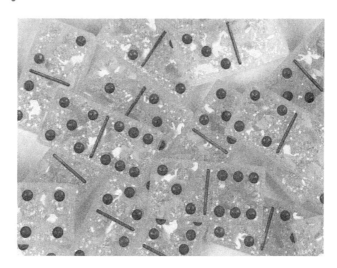

Dominos are not only fun to play with, but they also make a great decoration piece. Since childhood, I have always been obsessed with dominos, so I thought of making glittery transparent ones using this simple method.

Materials Required:

- Domino silicone molds
- Blending spoons
- Weighing cups
- A parchment paper sheet
- Resin and hardener liquids
- Gold leaf, dried flowers, or glitter
- Powdered pearl pigment
- 1 little brush and acrylic paint.

How to Make It:

Use your stirring sticks to thoroughly blend the liquid resin and hardener in a container such as a jug or measuring cup. For the right ratio, follow the directions on your bottle. Divide the combined resin into as many cups as are required to achieve the desired number of colors. You can also add some glitter. Pour a very thin coating of resin mixture into the bottom of the domino mold. Then, sprinkle glitter, gold leaf, or dried flowers into each domino mold. Fill each domino piece with the remaining resin mixture after you are satisfied with your decorations. Give it two to three days to set. Carefully remove the dominoes from the silicone mold once they have dried. Make dots on your dominoes using your little brush and acrylic paint.

12. Galaxy Painted Resin Clock

Do you want to make a wall hanging for your bedroom? Well, now you can convert some plain old clock into a fancy-looking galaxy-painted clock to revamp its look. You can add any set of colors to decorate the clock and make it match the theme of your living space.

Materials Required:

- Wood clock base
- Clockmaker hardware
- Clock numbers
- Pour-on resin
- Mixing cups
- Stirring sticks
- Gloves
- Worksurface
- Apple barrel paints in black, white, blue, pink, aqua, yellow
- E6000 glue

How to Make It:

Paint the entire clock base black with acrylic paint. Sprinkle yellow, pink, blue, and green glitter like stardust over the base. After that, lightly sprinkle white paint to make stars. Stick the clock's numbers on the base using glue. Then combine 2 ounces of high gloss resin in the mixing cups. After properly blending, pour the mixture onto the clock. The clock should be placed on a disposable surface and supported by a few plastic cups so the resin can drip out. Remove the bubbles, if any. The resin should then be left to cure for 24 hours. Attach the clock hands and other parts to their places. Your clock is ready to go up on a wall.

13. Glittery Unicorn Comb

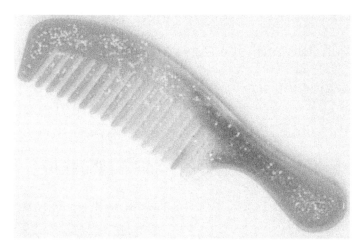

Here is a fancy way to style a plastic comb. This comb is an excellent gift for kids who want their dresser to look funky and colorful. The same idea can be used to make a monochromatic resin comb for yourself.

Materials Required:

- Clear epoxy resin
- Epoxy pigments in dark pink, orange, and turquoise
- Sparkling glitter
- Comb mold
- 3 plastic cups
- Popsicle stick

How to Make It:

Make sure that the color resins are combined in a volume ratio of 1 to 1. Blend the resin and hardener for this comb for 4 minutes in a paper cup with a popsicle stick. Split the colors evenly among the three paper cups after thoroughly combining them, and then add two drops of each colorant to each cup to create the pink, orange, and turquoise resin. Then add some iridescent glitter and stir it in.

Start by pouring the pink resin into the comb mold from one end, filling it to about one-third of the way down. Then add the turquoise resin, a little pinker resin, and the orange resin. Create a gradient swirl by slowly combining the colors with a popsicle stick. Then leave for 24 hours to cure and harden. Unmold the colorful rainbow comb after 24 hours. Again, leave it for 2-3 days to set completely.

14. Resin Heart Paperweights

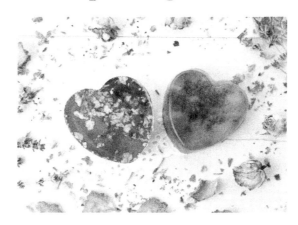

These heart-shaped paperweights are great for decorating your table and adding colors. You can use mini alphabet beads to add a message to these paperweights, or you can add several colors and give the hearts a 3D effect. I used confetti, gold leaf, and glitter to make mine.

Materials Required:

- Silicone heart molds
- Clear Resin kit
- Alphabet beads
- Toothpicks
- Confetti
- Glitter
- Dried flowers
- Gold leaf
- Alcohol ink
- Buttons

- Sequins

How to Make It:

Look for a resin craft kit or supplies at your neighborhood craft store if one exists. Most hobby shops and craft supply stores will have the essential supplies you want. If not, you can buy them online. I used letter beads to construct our paperweight resin craft to give the paperweights Valentine's Day conversation heart atmosphere. But there are many other things you can put to your resin paperweight!

Incorporate the resin as directed on the container. In a cup, combine resin and hardener in equal amounts. Stir for two minutes. Transfer to another cup and whisk for an additional two minutes.

Use smooth motions when stirring and avoid adding unnecessary air bubbles. The resin will remain as transparent as possible as a result. Add resin to the heart-shaped mold, about halfway full. Set your beads gently on the resin's surface, taking care to account for the backward letters; what you see on top of the resin will be the paperweight's reverse side.

The beads should descend to the ground. The beads could move as you add them and then let them sink to the bottom. To gently move them back into place, use a toothpick. Try not to let them touch and keep them hovering just above the bottom of the mold rather than pushing them to the bottom. As stated in the kit's instructions, let the resin set. Remove the paperweights from the molds once they have dried.

15. Resin Charcuterie Board

For this project, you can choose any board; there are no right or wrong choices here. Sturdy hardwoods like maple, walnut, cherry, or ash, cut in a cross-section slab with visible edges, are highly recommended. Choose a piece of wood that speaks to you, is the right size, and has the color and grain you like. A coat of resin is an excellent way to protect the wood's surface that still has its bark attached. You can add resin between the two split halves of the board or make a charcuterie board that is half wood and half resin. In any case, you can use the following technique to turn it into a masterpiece.

Materials Required:

- 1 piece of wood, cut in half
- Epoxy resin
- Nitrile gloves
- Level
- 1 measuring cup with easy-to-read measurement lines

- 1 mixing container

- 1 stir stick

- 1 spreader or popsicle stick

- 1 handheld torch

- Toothpicks

- 1 empty plastic tote or cardboard box

How to Make It:

Over your work surface, spread out a plastic drop cloth or shower curtain. Make sure your wood is leveled by supporting it on stands. Ensure that your dust cover box is nearby. Measure out precisely equal amounts of resin and hardener (by volume). Mix well for 3 minutes while scraping the sides and bottom of the mixing bowl. Onto the center of the board, pour and spread the resin. Spread it to the edges using a popsicle stick or a plastic spreader. Before the resin becomes too thick, you'll have around 45 minutes to work with it.

Use a torch to remove any bubbles from the resin. It must be cured for 24 hours, covered in a plastic bag or a cardboard box with the flaps cut off. You can sand away any drips once it has dried. To give the Charcuterie a fancy look, you can add colors, gold flakes, or glitter to the resin before pouring it over the board.

16. Epoxy Resin Night Lamp

Have you seen resin lamps lately? They are fascinating pieces of art, aren't they? I instantly fell in love with them when I first saw a glowing resin lamp at a shop. So, I thought of making one myself using resin, some led lights, and wooden skewers. For this lamp, I used the skewers from the kitchen to create a wooden base and a top wooden portion. The resin is filled and cured between the parts of the skewers. If you find this DIY lamp idea more complicated, you can create a simple one by creating a basic wooden base and a rectangular resin block with led lights resting on the wooden top.

Materials Required:

- 3 packets of wooden skewers
- Plastic sheet for mold container
- Glue
- Transparent epoxy resin
- Fairy string LED light
- Belt sander
- Hot glue
- Micro USB connector
- Battery for lights
- Danish oil for wood finish
- Sandpaper with 400, 800, 1000, and 1500 grit.
- Electric tape

- Drill and bits

- Clamps and some other usual bits and bobs

- Cutters

- Soldering iron

How to Make It:

To create this useful lamp, you'll need a lot of wooden skewers, epoxy glue, some plastic, and a few LEDs. Start by cutting those skewers in half after you have everything you need. The next step in any resin project is mold construction, which is one of the most important things to do. You'll need a rectangle mold with a hole on one side to hold the power source. Measuring and pasting plastic panels together is the simplest way to build this mold. Take 3 (1-foot-long x ½ foot wide) plastic panels for the sides and two ½ x ½ foot panels for the top and bottom. Stick their edges together to make a rectangular box. This rectangle must be placed on the working surface with its long open side facing upward. Drill a small hole into the base of this box.

This makeshift container will let you arrange skewers on both sides, the top, and the bottom. Ensure that the skewers are tightly packed so that both sides resemble solid pieces of wood. You must fasten the bundle of sticks once you've placed them to keep them from shifting. To do so, stick two small plastic panels at the base and bottom of the box. And keep the tips of the skewers towards the center part of the rectangle. Insert the led string from the center of the skewers through the hole left in the plastic-based mold. Keep the lights plug out of the mold, seal this hole with glue, and let it harden before adding the resin. Stick a metallic or plastic base under the bottom layer of this mold to create a support for the lamp.

Finally, after the preparation, the resin can be added to the mold. You may make your lamp using any color you like. Mix the resin and hardener in a 3-liter container. Stir in the pigment of your preference and mix well for 3 minutes. Pour the resin into the mold and remove all the bubbles. Allow the resin to cure for 2-3 days, then remove the plastic panels.

Take the lamp to a belt sander and sand it to ensure that the shape is even throughout. Your lamp will appear somewhat dull and opaque after the sanding process, so be sure to buffer and polish it to restore some of its transparency. The LEDs should shine through if you buffer and polish the lamp properly and brighten the space with the color of the resin of your choice. Place it on a side table and plug it in.

The bad thing about resin-encasing LEDs is that the lights will ultimately stop working and burn out. They cannot be changed without cutting the resin altogether. While the lighting is still good, you can use this lamp to add an enchanting glow to your workspace or area.

17. Easy Terrarium Diorama

Nothing beats the look of a customized homemade diorama you make using your artsy skills. This terrarium diorama has an underwater look with a central rock, attached plants, and miniature fish inside. Using other tiny objects, you can use the same concept to style your diorama the way you want.

Materials Required:

- Square diorama mold
- Clear epoxy resin
- Blue and green pigment
- Plaster of Paris
- Acrylic colors
- Miniature plants and fish
- Artificial grass

How to Make It:

This method of making a diorama can be used to make any possible version. You can change the pigments and the inclusions to create a different effect. I wanted to create an underwater look for this one, so here is how it is done.

Create a shape of a base rock by folding an aluminum foil sheet into the desired shape. Cover this rock with some plaster from Paris and let it dry off. Once dried, you can color the rock dark brown using acrylic paints and then give the effect of moss and greenery on top using other shades of green. You can attach different parts of the terrarium, like a miniature tree on this rock.

Now prepare the epoxy resin by mixing its two parts per the packaging instructions. Add blue and green pigments into the resin and just stir to create swirls of two colors mixing. Place the rock and grass at the bottom of the mold. Pour ½ of the resin, add some miniature fish on top of this layer then pour another layer on top. Remove the bubbles, if any, then leave the diorama to dry for 24 hours. Remove it from the mold, then let it cure for 2-3 days. Use sandpaper to add a finish to the surfaces. Apply polish and spread it evenly. Let it dry before using.

18. Wooden Resin Table

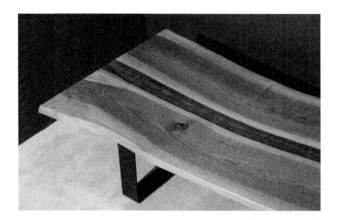

Wooden resin tables with that river flowing effect cost you a fortune if you buy them from a furniture shop. The good news is that you can make one yourself in your workshop using the right raw materials. In this way, you will only have to invest in the supplies, and in turn, you will get a great-looking table with your customized tabletop just the way you want it.

Materials Required:

- Clear epoxy resin
- Wood - English Yew, with a waney edge
- Blue translucent tinting pigments
- Flash/release and double-sided tape
- Polypropylene Sheet
- Polishing compound and oil
- Abrasive paper
- Spreader and mixing sticks
- Mixing cups and mixing buckets

- Epoxy Adhesive

- Safety Equipment

- Hot-melt glue-gun

How to Make It:

When selecting your wood, ensure it is level, dry, and as seasoned as possible. Although unique textures and waney-edges are ideal for this craft, the style and type of wood are a matter of personal preference. Experts usually prepare and cut out the piece of wood by themselves, but if you don't have the necessary tools, you can simply buy it. Ask the retailer to cut the wood in half if you plan to build a central river channel. Remove the bark with a chisel, then use abrasive paper to remove any remaining debris. Wipe or vacuum the wood to remove any remaining dust and filth.

The next step is to look for gaps, cracks, and knotholes on the top and bottom of the wood pieces and fill them with resin to seal them. To stop the resin from leaking out of the cracks and openings, use some tape to seal them; release tape works well. Fill in any open spaces with a tiny amount of resin that has been measured, mixed, and applied; check on this after a few hours to see if more resin needs to be added because the wood will likely absorb part of it. Use abrasives to level off the surface when the resin has fully cured. You should remove any high areas with a sander or abrasive paper since you want to get an even surface to work with.

The resin can be measured by volume at a ratio of 2:1 resin to hardener. Start by placing a flat sheet of chipboard on the working surfaces that are just slightly larger than the table top you will create. Cover this chipboard with a polypropylene sheet, then place your wood slabs on this sheet while leaving room for the river channel between the wood.

Then, cut the side walls of the mold from another polypropylene sheet because the resin doesn't stick to it and build a good container around the wood. Place the side barriers around the wooden planks inside their rectangular frame. Secure the polypropylene frame by gluing their edges together and place long batons of chipboard wood around this frame.

Use clamps or weights to keep the planks in place; test the resin to ensure it stays as flat as possible. You can remove all the supports and clamps later when you're satisfied. Cover the side batons with flash/release tape to prevent them from sticking to the resin.

Using a blue translucent tinting pigment creates a watery look on our table. To complete this job, divide the primary river pour into two sections and pour a base/sealing layer first. A total of 10 kg of prepared resin is required for this project. So first weigh out 5 kg of resin and add a few drops of the color pigment to the resin at a time and thoroughly mix.

You will need 1.6kg of the resin hardener mixture for each resin layer. So, mix the pre-colored resin thoroughly after adding the appropriate amount of hardener. Add this mixture to another clean bucket and stir once more. Use 1.6 kg of the resin liquid for every layer added to the tabletop. Pour the mixture into the polypropylene frame without the wood planks. Spread this layer evenly, and the resin must cover the entire base. Reposition the wood planks so that they are in the proper place. Seal the edge and top surface with resin using a brush, making sure to fill any open wooden spaces, splits, or knots. Place tape-covered wood blocks over the barriers and batons and secure them using clamps. Let the resin cure the B-stage. The B-stage denotes that the resin has begun to set but is still tacky.

With a gloved finger, touch the resin to see if this stage has been achieved. If it doesn't stick to the glove, it has reached its B stage, and part 1 of the pour needs to be prepared. If you let the resin cure past the B stage, it won't chemically attach to the next layer and must be keyed with abrasive paper all over to forge a bond with the new layer.

You must have the resin ready for Layer 1 after the base/sealing layer reaches the B-stage. Measure the pre-pigmented resin and the appropriate quantity of hardener, then combine. Transfer to a second bucket and stir once more. Resin should be poured into the river channel. You can speed up curing by using a heat gun or hairdryer on a medium heat held back from the resin. Use a heat gun to remove any bubbles. Allow Layer 1 to cure till the B-stage. Once the B-stage of part 1 has been achieved, repeat the processes for the second main pour.

Repeat the procedure as necessary to fill the river. While pouring multiple layers, wait until the B-stage is reached before mixing and pouring the next layer. Ensure the river channel is somewhat overfilled, then give the resin time to cure fully. Leave it for one week to cure completely. Remove the molds. Then use wet sandpaper or an electric polisher to polish the table's surface. Apple the polish oil on top and apply it evenly. Let it dry and attach the tabletop to a frame of legs using screws, drill, nuts, etc. Your table is now ready to use!

CONCLUSION

Resin art is one of the most satisfying crafts you will ever come across in your life. Using a few simple materials, you can create some fantastic lamps, tables, dioramas, and whatnot. If you are a teensy bit interested in this art form, you should try it and start by working on smaller projects like making a little resin pendant or a serving tray.

Working on beginner-level projects helps you learn how to mix and pour the resin and wait until it completes its curing time. With more experience, you can jump to your next big project, like crafting a river table or making enchanting lamps.

In this book, I have tried to summarize all the necessary details for every beginner to get started with their resin artwork. You can, too, pick your favorite DIY project from the collection and start making one right away. Good luck and have tons of fun!

Printed in Great Britain
by Amazon

84383310R00052